SWITZERLAND

A PICTURE MEMORY

Text
Bill Harris

Captions
Laura Potts

Design
Teddy Hartshorn

Photography
Prisma, Zürich

Commissioning Editor
Andrew Preston

Editorial
David Gibbon

Director of Production
Gerald Hughes

CLB 2927
© 1993 CLB Publishing, Godalming, Surrey
All rights reserved
This 1993 edition published by Magna Books,
Magna Road, Wigston, Leicester LE18 4ZH
Printed and bound in Singapore
ISBN 1-85422-575-8

SWITZERLAND

A PICTURE MEMORY

MAGNA
BOOKS

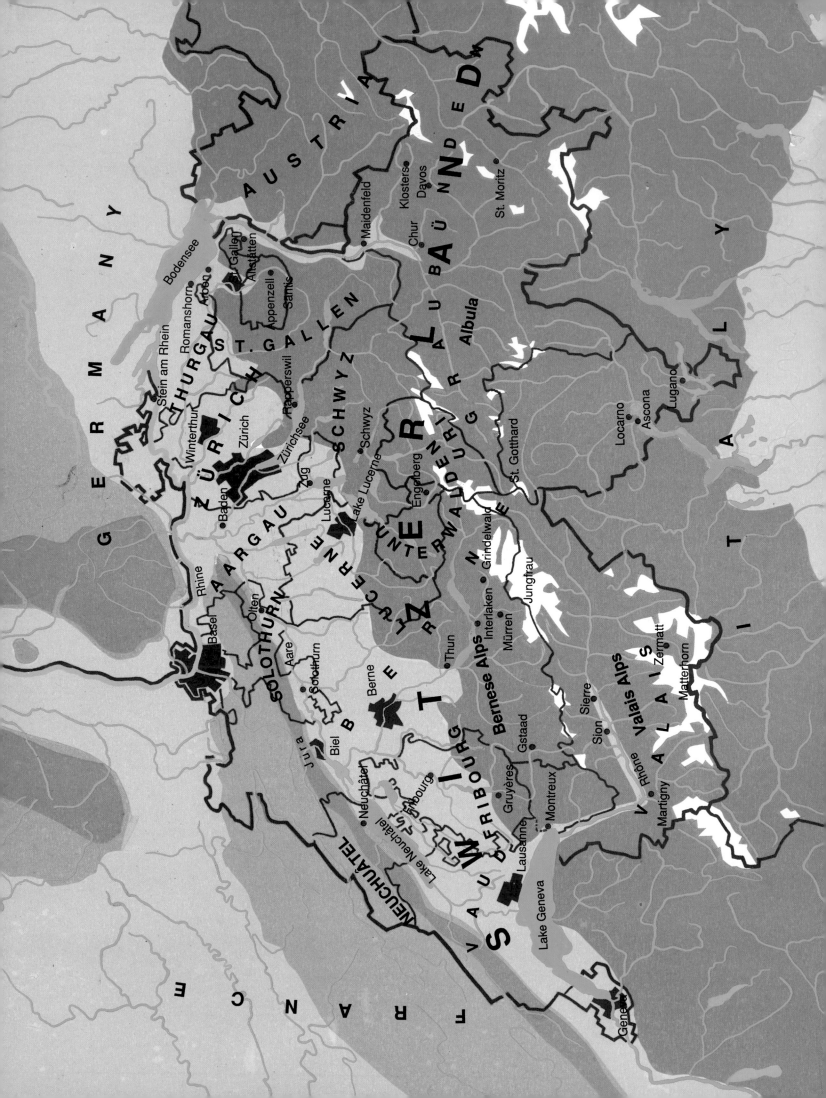

Of all the things everyone knows about Switzerland, the most often mentioned is its dedication to neutrality when nearly all the other countries of the world seem to be constantly planning to destroy one another. Yet the national symbol of this country is a crossbow. It appears on everything, from wheels of cheeses to boxes of chocolate, but this is no ordinary crossbow. It represents the one that belonged to William Tell.

His story, whether true or not, has its beginnings in the eleventh and twelfth centuries, when the Swiss were ruled by nobles from Germany and Austria. In 1291, three of the cantons, Uri, Unterwalden and Schwyz, the namesake of the modern country, signed a secret pact pledging to fight for their independence from the Austrian Hapsburgs, whose own ancestors were Swiss themselves, but who had no scruples about oppressing them. The fight was a quiet one, but it was enough to unnerve the Austrian governor, a tyrant named Gessler, and he decided it was time to test the people's loyalty. It was an easy test that anyone could avoid with a wink and crossed fingers, because all Gessler required was that anyone passing through the marketplace in Altdorf should remove their hat and bow to a symbolic hat he had nailed to a post there. One of the citizens of Uri, however, the archer William Tell, would have none of it, and one day as he marched past the makeshift Austrian shrine with his hat squarely on his head he was arrested and taken to the governor to explain himself. Even in the presence of his would-be master, Tell still refused to remove his hat, and the furious Gessler sentenced him to pay for the affront by shooting an apple from his young son's head. When Tell arrived to comply with the sentence he had two arrows with him, one of which he used to slice the apple neatly in two without disturbing a hair on the boy's head. When Gessler asked him what the second arrow was for, William Tell told him that if his son had died, it was intended to end the miserable life of the governor himself. Charging him with an assassination plot, Gessler arrested Tell and chained him to a boat that would take him across Lake Lucerne to spend the rest of his life in a dungeon. The boat carrying the governor, his guards and their prisoner had barely left the shore when a violent storm came up. Knowing that William Tell was as handy with a boat as with a crossbow, the soldiers begged the Gessler to release

the prisoner and, when he agreed, Tell brought the boat under control and headed for shore. Before reaching the safety of the beach he jumped overboard with his bow and arrows and disappeared into the forest, leaving the Austrians to row for their lives. Gessler, it turned out, didn't have much longer to live. The next day he was ambushed at Küssnacht and was killed with the arrow William Tell had been saving for him.

Usually such stories have stirring endings, with the people rallying behind the hero and driving the oppressors from their land. Such was not the case with William Tell. He went back to his old life in the forest and, according to legend, lived to become a very old man, finally meeting his end attempting to save a boy from drowning. In the meantime, the hated Gessler was replaced by another of the Hapsburg minions and, for a while at least, not much changed. But the pact that had united the three cantons was still in place, and a dozen years after it was signed, it was countersigned by the emperor in Vienna and, on paper at least, the three Swiss communities had their rights confirmed. In 1315, though, Duke Leopold of Hapsburg decided it represented a dangerous precedent and sent a 20,000-strong army to destroy the town of Schwyz and show the people who was boss. It wasn't a good idea. When the soldiers arrived at the field of Morgarten, a few miles north of the town, they were ambushed by a small but fierce peasant army armed with hoes, clubs, and homemade spears. The battle began with an avalanche of boulders and uprooted trees, and ended with the disorderly retreat of the invaders. Back in Vienna, it was made quite clear who was boss in the land that until that day had been known as Helvetia, but now called itself Switzerland, and it was just as clear in the Helvetian mountains and forests. Gradually, other cantons joined the original three, and by the middle of the 14th century eight of them were bound together in a confederation pledged to resist any attempts at rule by outsiders.

Naturally the Hapsburgs didn't take it lying down, and for nearly two hundred years Switzerland was in an almost constant state of war with them. The Swiss won more battles than they lost, though, and developed an enviable reputation as the best fighters in Europe, as well as an image of fierce devotion to independence.

The Hapsburgs finally bowed to the inevitable in 1394 and formally gave up their Swiss lands, authorizing the cantons to maintain an army of 100,000 men who would be their allies rather than their enemies. What had been a defending army up until then was used over the next century to expand territory, and because it was an arm of the whole Confederation and not of any one canton, it cemented the eight into a kind of nation.

The Confederation was, however, still far from united. Growing trade made the towns prosperous, but farmers and herders weren't sharing the wealth, and tensions between city people and country people were threatening to tear the union apart from the inside. The internal rivalries came to a head after the Swiss joined with Austria and France to defeat the kingdom of Burgundy in 1477, and added the western Canton of Vaud to the map of Switzerland. A short time later Fribourg and Solothurn asked to join the Confederation, but the farm-oriented communities refused them out of fear that the already shaky balance between urban and rural interests would be destroyed.

The impasse was broken by a hermit farmer, Nicholas von der Flüe, who reasoned with the Swiss leaders and convinced them that compromise was their only salvation. He suggested that Switzerland should become the nation it already resembled, rather than remain a confederation of independent city-states, and that they should work together as a single unit. Fribourg and Solothurn were admitted to the league on the condition of their promise to act as mediators, and Basle, Schaffhausen and Appenzell were soon welcomed on the same terms. In his quiet way the hermit Nicholas had become the father of modern Switzerland, and eventually he was designated the country's patron saint.

But if the Swiss nation was fathered by a saint, the gods of war still had a strong influence. When the French attacked Italy in 1492, the Swiss were in the thick of it, fighting as mercenaries on both sides and eventually fighting with one another over which side was right. The division opened the door for the French, who defeated the Swiss two decades later and forced a treaty of perpetual peace from them. For the French it meant nearly exclusive use of Swiss troops for their own army, but for the Swiss it was a sobering experience. From then on, they decided, the best way to protect themselves as a small nation at the crossroads of Europe was to stay neutral in international disputes.

Still, they had a reputation for producing the best soldiers in the world, and they were still willing to fight for anyone who would pay for their services. They always signed on as units, insisting on marching among their countrymen behind their own officers, no matter whose flag they carried. Until 1874, when the constitution outlawed the practice, these fighting units were Switzerland's most important export. The only survival of Switzerland's mercenary troops is the 110-man Swiss Guard that has served as the pope's protectors in the Vatican since 1505.

Strict neutrality was a unique idea in the 16th century, and the Swiss were often called upon to fight for their right to stay out of other people's wars. Yet for the most part their reputation made invaders think twice about crossing the mountains to attack them, and Switzerland eventually evolved into a peaceful center of culture. Other forces, however, were at work in Europe at the time, and they threatened the existence of the united cantons in ways no foreign army could. The Protestant Reformation didn't begin in Switzerland, but Switzerland became one of the great battlegrounds in the war for men's souls.

Switzerland was one of the oldest Christian lands in Europe, with traditions dating back to its days under Roman rule, and Irish Catholic missionaries had reinforced their beliefs with massive conversions in the fifth century. When the new Protestants were driven from their own countries, many migrated to neutral Switzerland, and became the spearhead of a new missionary movement. Their calls for reform had a special appeal for city people, who believed the Catholic church was holding them back, and that in turn made the people in rural areas, always suspicious of the urban elite, more Catholic than ever. Old divisions, heightened by religious fervor, resurfaced but sadly this time around there was no saint waiting in the wings to pour oil on troubled waters.

One man some considered had the qualities of a saint was Ulrich Zwingli, a Zürich priest who began preaching against the sale of indulgences as a means of shortening the route to heaven. When he formed his own church and started calling for an end to profiting from military service, many who had been living on those profits drifted even further into the Catholic camp. Opposition to Zwingli and his converts became intense when he suggested that the government ought to be reorganized and power centered in Berne and Zürich, and in 1531 it boiled over into an open war. The Protestants were soundly beaten and Zwingli killed for his beliefs. The Catholic victory didn't mean the end of religious toleration in Switzerland, although the winners did manage to gain control of the government. In fact, the country's reputation for openness encouraged even more Protestants to relocate there. Among them was John Calvin, who had been banished from France for his controversial ideas, and he established himself in Geneva to develop his beliefs and to win new converts. Eventually the city became the world's most influential center of Protestantism, and missionaries based there carried Calvin's message across Europe from Hungary to Scotland.

Not everyone in Switzerland accepted the new faith. When the Counter-Reformation began sweeping across Europe in the 1550s the Swiss Catholics took it as a sign to reassert themselves, and many cantons found themselves torn apart through long years of religious wars. The result was a kind of stagnation that lasted well into the 18th century. The constitution remained unchanged even though the needs of the country were different, and no new cantons were added because of a concern that the balance of religious power would be altered. Even traditional oaths, by which men bound themselves together, couldn't be used because they usually called upon the saints to guide them. Such an idea was unacceptable to the Protestants, but changing the wording was out of the question for the Catholics. Eventually the government itself was split in two, with one parliament for the Catholics and another for the Protestants. The situation not only had an effect on the Swiss people themselves, but it allowed foreign governments to deal with whichever faction was more likely to give them what they wanted.

Apart from civil wars and a helpless government, Switzerland also changed culturally. In Catholic areas baroque art and architecture flourished, but in Protestant cities restraint was the order of the day. But if Switzerland was divided, most of the economic power was in the hands of the Protestants, and as time went on their money gave them access to the lion's share of the political power. The situation was finally resolved in the wake of the American and French revolutions which began to show other countries that change was possible if people were willing to fight for it. In 1798 the citizens of Vaud attacked the Bernese army that was occupying their land, and proclaimed a new republic. This republic was short-lived. The French took this opportunity to attack, and three months later its army took control of the new Republic of Vaud, soon after capturing all of Switzerland and renaming it the Helvetic Republic.

The independent-minded Swiss obviously didn't welcome their new masters, and by the time Napoleon took charge it had become a thorn in the French side. Five years after it was created he abolished the Helvetic Republic and changed it to what he called a federal regime, with power centered in the hands of a chief known as the Landammann. On the surface it seemed better than the divided government the Swiss had lived under before the French arrived, but still not all of the people were pleased. Change came in 1815, when the Congress of Vienna re-addressed the balance of power in Europe after Napoleon's defeat. It reconfirmed Swiss neutrality and recognized the country's independence, and after five centuries Switzerland's borders were finally defined.

But they weren't out of the woods yet.

The new order of things was quite remarkably similar to the state of affairs that existed at first. Although their constitution had given them a parliament, Switzerland was again a collection of communities, each with its own laws and customs and little regard for any central authority. The social revolution that swept Europe in 1840s gave the Swiss an opportunity to get rid of the old elite and reassert individual rights, but the problem of religious differences still remained. After seven Catholic cantons broke away from the union to form an alliance they called the Sonderbund, for mutual protection, a short-lived civil war broke out in 1847. It lasted less than a month and cost just 150 lives, but when it was over the road was paved for the adoption of a new constitution that radically changed the way Switzerland was run.

Power in the central government was divided between two houses: one representing the people and the other the cantons. The individual states still kept their authority, but the new scheme forced them to share it with the federal government. The Protestants and the Catholics were still wary of one another, but eventually they worked out their differences, partly because of the prosperity their neutrality brought, and by the 1890s new reforms turned the country into a sophisticated democracy.

And then the sun came out. Although Switzerland had been a required stop on every Grand Tour of Europe in the 18th and 19th centuries, travelers worried that they might find themselves caught up in a revolution or a civil war before moving on to the next stop. Neutrality had always seemed like a strange concept to outsiders, but in the 1860s and '70s, when Europe was a hotbed of intrigue, the Swiss proved that they wouldn't take sides with any other powers, no matter what the stakes, and made it clear they wouldn't stand for any outsiders using their territory. Suddenly it dawned on the rest of the world that the Swiss meant what they said. If they were having trouble getting their act together at home, it was their problem and it was being worked out.

And once it was worked out they began reaching out. In the 1860s Henri Dunant formed the International Red Cross, with its headquarters in Geneva. Its Swiss origins were confirmed a year later, when the other countries of Europe agree that its symbol should be a red cross on a white field – the Swiss flag with its colors reversed – and it has ever since been a sign of help. Dunant also headed the first meeting to discuss the rules of war, the Geneva Conference of 1864, which provided the first guidelines in the history of warfare for humane treatment of prisoners. Sixteen countries ratified the original treaty, and later versions of it have been signed by virtually every power in the world.

After World War I the Swiss joined the League of Nations, which was headquartered at Geneva, but when the United Nations was formed, its concept of providing selective security for the world made it impossible for Switzerland to be neutral and a UN member at the same time. But the Swiss are solid members of dozens of United Nations relief organizations, several of which are based in Geneva, and they are active around the world in other peaceful pursuits. Their embassies are frequently the representatives of friendly governments in not-so-friendly countries, and they are often the middlemen who make a difference when other nations would rather not speak directly to one another.

And although the Swiss have been known for centuries as the world's most formidable fighters, they have managed to live in uninterrupted peace through times when the rest of the world seemed bent on destroying itself. It is a wonderful means of fulfilling a prophecy made more than a century ago by the French writer Victor Hugo, who said "In history, Switzerland will have the last word."

Facing page: the rich colors of fall bring an added dimension to the landscape of the Jura, in northwestern Switzerland.

In the spring and summer wildflowers (above) bloom in abundance and the vines, like those at Aigle (top left), are thick with leaves. Geraniums flower in window boxes, bringing additional charm to historic towns like Gruyères (below), and flags, like those in Delémont (center left), fly proudly in most towns. Bottom left: Château de Chillon. Facing page top: the ancient city of Fribourg. Facing page bottom: the town of Neuchâtel. Overleaf: the village of Fechy and Lake Geneva.

The Water Jet (below), which reaches a height of 400 feet and can be seen from miles around, is one of Geneva's best-known landmarks. The city is the largest and most important of the elegant towns found on the northern shores of Lake Geneva. Lausanne – perched above the waterfront district of Ouchy (facing page bottom) – and Montreux (facing page top) are among the most popular of these lakeside towns. Overleaf: Lake Geneva and the Mont Blanc Bridge by night.

The Rhone Valley, from Lake Geneva to the Rhone Glacier, is encompassed by the Valais (these pages), the third largest canton in Switzerland. Temperatures in the valley, which is protected from the harsh winds by the surrounding mountains, are mild, and vines, like those near Sierre (right), flourish. The canton boasts the lovely cities of Sion (below) and Martigny (center right), as well as charming villages such as Goms (bottom right). Overleaf: a view of Sion and the Rhone Valley.

Fine ski resorts such as Morgins (facing page top) and Bettmeralp (facing page bottom) are found in the Valais Alps. The Matterhorn (below) – the magnificent, triangular-shaped peak located in the Upper Valais – is one of Switzerland's best-known landmarks and is undoubtedly the canton's most popular tourist attraction. Snow covers the slopes right through until April, offering some fine skiing. Overleaf: the peaceful resort town of Zermatt, with the Matterhorn beyond.

The breathtaking scenery in the Bernese Oberland (these pages) has long been an inspiration for writers and musicians. Lovely waterfalls, like Staubbach Falls (above), are characteristic of Lauterbrunnen valley. From the town of Grindelwald (bottom left) there are lovely views of the surrounding peaks, including the Eiger (below) and the Wetterhorn (top left). Facing page top: the funicular at Mürren. Facing page bottom: the resort of Gstaad. Overleaf: the Lauterbrunnen valley.

Kleine Scheidegg (below), in the Bernese Oberland, though particularly popular in winter, is a year-round resort, with trips on the famous Jungfrau Railway – an engineering marvel that tunnels through the Eiger and Mönch mountains, climbing a total of 4,200 feet – starting here. Facing page top: magnificent scenery near Mürren. Facing page bottom: a train makes its winding journey through the Schynige Platte, in the Bernese Oberland. Overleaf: the Eiger, Mönch, and Jungfrau soar above the clouds.

Interlaken (facing page top), a world-famous beauty spot, stands between lakes Thun and Brienz. Around the shores of Lake Thun, the larger and deeper of the two, stand the beautiful towns of Thun (below and center left), located at the tip of the lake, Spiez (facing page bottom) on its southern shore, and Oberhofen – which boasts a twelfth-century castle (bottom left) – on its northern shore. Above: the town square in Biel. Top left: the fountain in Büren's town square.

The city of Berne (these pages), the seat of government of the Swiss Confederation, was founded in 1191. Its location, on a rocky peninsula above the River Aare (facing page top), was chosen by the city's founder, the Duke of Zähringen, because of its strategic importance. The Clock Tower (above) and Justice Fountain (below) are the most famous of Berne's landmarks. The old town is dominated by the cathedral (top right and facing page bottom). Center right: the Bundeshaus.

Basle (these pages), in northwestern Switzerland, stands at a crossroads in Europe, a position that has long ensured its prosperity. The city, which is home to the headquarters of the influential Bank for International Settlements (left), is renowned as one of Europe's major banking and insurance centers. Its commercial importance, however, should not overshadow its historical significance. Built on the banks of the Rhine (below), and surveyed by its twin-spired cathedral (facing page), the city boasts a unique blend of medieval charm and 20th century prosperity. Overleaf: the pretty village of Häfelfingen, in the sub-canton of Basle-Land.

The canton of Aargau, in northern Switzerland, boasts some lovely historic towns, including Aarburg (below), Laufenburg (facing page top), and Baden (facing page bottom). Though Baden is known principally as a spa town, and is famous for its mineral-rich hot springs, it also offers other attractions. The medieval quarter of the city is particularly well preserved, and is noted for the covered bridge, which crosses the River Limmat, leading to the Bailiff's Castle.

Lucerne (above and facing page bottom), located on the shores of Lake Lucerne, was referred to by Alexandre Dumas as "a pearl in the world's most beautiful oyster." The Kapellbrücke (facing page top), a lovely fourteenth-century covered bridge, has become one of the symbols of the city. Steamers travel the lake, visiting attractive lakeside towns such as Weggis (center right), and Beckenried (top right). Below: A Pro Castle, near Seedorf. Bottom right: Engelberg, in Obwalden.

Through the heart of Zurich (these pages) – Switzerland's largest city, renowned the world over as an international center for banking and commerce – flows the shallow River Limmat (top left). The river is bordered on both sides by attractive quays, such as Limmat Quai (below). Most views of the city are dominated by the copper-domed towers of the Grossmünster (bottom left), the church where the influential Protestant reformer Ulrich Zwingli preached. Center left: Bahnhofstrasse.

The Munot (facing page top), a circular fortress, dominates the town of Schaffhausen. The canton of Schaffhausen offers attractions such as the Rheinfall (facing page bottom) and pretty towns like Stein am Rhein (below). The canton of Thurgau, like Schaffhausen, borders Lake Constance. Lakeside towns include Arbon (top right and bottom right) and Steckborn (center right). Above: elaborate facades on Kolinplatz in the town of Zug. Overleaf: rolling landscape in the canton of Zug.

Rorschach (top left) on Lake Constance, and Rapperswil (bottom left) on Lake Zurich, are two charming towns in the canton of St. Gallen. The canton's capital, also named St. Gallen (below), is dominated by the towers of its baroque cathedral. The town of Altstätten (center left) stands near the boundary with Appenzell, a small canton famed for pretty villages like Gais (above). Facing page top: the town of Glarus. Facing page bottom: Obstalden, overlooking Walensee.

Appenzell, in northeastern Switzerland, is a small canton located entirely within the boundaries of St. Gallen. The scenery around Säntis (below) – the region's highest peak – is superb, revealing the beauty of this remote part of Switzerland. The summit of the mountain is only accessible by cable car (facing page top), which runs throughout the year. The annual Landsgemeinde, or election, is held in Appenzell (facing page bottom), the canton's capital. Overleaf: rich farmland near Alt St. Johann.

Lugano (below and center left) deserves its reputation as one of Switzerland's most beautiful cities. Built on the shores of Lake Lugano, around a large picturesque bay, it, like other cities in Ticino – Switzerland's most southerly and only entirely Italian speaking canton – combines Italian charm with Swiss efficiency and orderliness. Ascona (top left and bottom left) is an attractive resort town on Lake Maggiore.

Chur (facing page bottom) is the capital of the Grisons, Switzerland's largest canton. The region is a popular winter playground, with resorts like glamourous St. Moritz (above), quietly exclusive Klosters (top right), and friendly Arosa (facing page top), as well as attractive villages like Splügen (center right) and Maienfeld (bottom right). Below: Darvella. Overleaf: Savognin, a pleasant low-key winter sports resort. Following page: a panoramic view near Salouf in the Grisons.